T0129011

Our *Poignant* Journey

A Journey That Opened
Up Our Hearts

Our *Poignant*
Journey

LORAINNE S. KAISER

OUR POIGNANT JOURNEY
A JOURNEY THAT OPENED UP OUR HEARTS

iUniverse books may be ordered through booksellers or by contacting:

iUniverse
1663 Liberty Drive
Bloomington, IN 47403
www.iuniverse.com
1-800-Authors (1-800-288-4677)

Because of the dynamic nature of the Internet, any web addresses or links contained in this book may have changed since publication and may no longer be valid. The views expressed in this work are solely those of the author and do not necessarily reflect the views of the publisher, and the publisher hereby disclaims any responsibility for them.

Any people depicted in stock imagery provided by Getty Images are models, and such images are being used for illustrative purposes only. Certain stock imagery © Getty Images.

Scripture taken from the King James Version of the Bible. Public Domain

ISBN: 978-1-5320-4810-4 (sc)
ISBN: 978-1-5320-4811-1 (e)

Print information available on the last page.

iUniverse rev. date: 05/25/2018

Contents

Foreword

Today many years have passed since the beginning of this crisis of disease and acrimony. This book is not meant to be controversial. Brian, my youngest son, died of AIDS in 1992. I am sharing my family's journey of love in hopes that it will help others.

The purpose of this book is to enlighten people, to experience fully the great capacity of loving hearts, and to know that all of life's lessons are to lead us to that purpose. Life is a process, not a result. This is a book directed at all families in our society; as all people either have been or will be affected by AIDS sometime in their lives. We will all need more loving hearts, more tolerance, more compassion - and less judgment.

CHAPTER 1

The Beginning

I was born in Detroit in 1928 to German parents who migrated to the USA. My father, who served in the German army, earned an apprenticeship as a furrier and came to America in 1923.

My mother, an only child, came to America nine months later. She supported his business at the fur store, in addition to being a terrific homemaker. There was a great deal of discipline and great strength and entrepreneurship, coming to a new land as young married people full of dreams and aspiration. They were hard working and made many sacrifices to make their dreams come true. This background helped me to become self-reliant at an early age. At 10, I began helping in my father's store, which gave me a feeling for business. At 15, I began managing an office while attending school for accounting. While finalizing my degree at the Detroit Business Institute, I met Brian's father, Albert. Albert was born in 1923, in Detroit also, the eldest of two sons. His parents traveled a lot, leaving him home with housekeepers, so we both understood self reliance. Albert had asthma as a child but with great desire and self-discipline he overcame the affliction.

Albert's father, one of nine children, was born on a farm in Michigan, left home at an early age and began working in factories, eventually became a manager till he decided to start up a manufacturing company of his own. He worked very hard also, out of his home at first, then moving into a large building where he supplied automobile companies with protector parts for the assembly lines. This business grew and Brian's father became manager and then owner of the family business.These early days were evidence of the pioneer spirit of hard work.

The Germanic influences were very strong in both our family ancestry; both of our upbringings were very strict and we internalized cloistered attitudes. We were trained as children to fit into existing social structures, roles, and behavior patterns.

After Brian's father and I met at business college, we married and became proud parents of two beautiful sons, born six years apart.

Robert, our first born, came to us two years into our marriage in August 1950. It was wonderful to have a boy, a boy to carry on the family name. He was so special to our parents too, especially mine since I was a girl and an only child. My mother was the perfect grandparent, showering much love and affection on him. As for Albert's parents, Robert was the first boy in the family, heir to the family name. They too showered much attention on him. He was a very creative child with many talents, we would learn later.

For a child to have loving grandparents is a great blessing. They can impact stability and bring maturity to the new family.

Then came Brian, six years later; it was like having two separate families.I had some health challenges and had almost given up hope of having a second child. Brian entered our lives in October 1956.

Having children is truly a gift from God. As an only child, I felt truly blessed to have two. I believe we are spirits housed in our structural bodies and that we come into life as God's universal caretakers, choosing our parents for the lessons we must learn. Parenthood is a joy, the growth process for both child and parent.

Brian was conceived in great love, as was Robert, and our journey through life was so enriched by our growing family. Brian was a happy child, outgoing, full of smiles, endearing all those who came into his path. He made friends easily, charming them with his radiant smile. He related well to people of all ages. He adored his brother and tried so hard to emulate him. His journey to discover himself was difficult. For the most part of his young life he seemed happy, at least I, as his mother, thought so. He had many friends and did well in school. He didn't excel with high grades, but seemed attentive and open to learning.

He tried to put on the cloak of a normal life, having girlfriends and going to his high school prom in great style, limousine and all. But we were to learn later he had discovered his homosexuality. We had suspected, but his father and I tried not to acknowledge it. Our love was being tested.

Brian attended University of Michigan prior to our move to Florida, and then transferred to Stetson University, where he received a bachelor degree in finance; upon graduation, he became a stockbroker. He was successful but discovered he was too invested in people's personal savings to continue as an broker and decided to become a wholesale stockbroker, selling only to brokerage firms. Things became difficult with his employment because of relationships and he decided to move to San Francisco. As we were a close family, this was a difficult decision for him to make and, of course, was hard for us to accept. He would be so far away from us all. In retrospect, this was the best decision for him, as he could accept his orientation by living anonymity. He had confided in his brother and sister-in-law and they kept his secret for several years.

The move was good for him. He found happiness there, but it was difficult for us all to be so far away. He and his brother, who still resides in Michigan, had a good relationship and they spoke often, with long conversations on the phone. Robert, with his car phone, would drive around the block avoiding the entrance into his garage. Robert finally told Brian that the time had come to tell mom and dad.

CHAPTER 2

The Revelation

Brian wrote a letter to tell us of his sexual orientation, but he couldn't bring himself to mail it. It was important to him for us to hear the news in the proper place. We were coming to visit him in San Francisco, and he found a beautiful bed and breakfast for us to stay - a lovely room with blue chintz wallpaper and drapes, a bay window, and a book-shelved fireplace.

He stood in front of us and tearfully read the letter he had prepared for us. I guess his tears were his fright as to how we would accept this revelation. Because he was such a considerate, compassionate man, he made every effort to present the revelation in a thoughtful and gentle manner. He was focused on our feelings and how much this news would hurt us. The process of acknowledging his orientation was difficult enough for him, and how to share this with us was extremely hard for him. I'm sure the moments before our response must have seemed an eternity.

This could have been a tragic day; it could have ended our relationship as it has for many young men and women and their parents. But my mate, his father Albert, was very loving and understanding and let him know we still loved and cared for him as much as before he told us. Although saddened by this disclosure, I could only feel love and concern for this our youngest son.

Dear Mom and Dad:

It is April and I am already looking forward to your visit. I am anxious to show you both the many things I appreciate about living in this city and also to share something important about myself too! I think the time is now right and so by now you know that I am both emotionally and physically attracted to men. I believe I understand how disturbing my confirmation of my sexuality will be to you. My own journey to understand myself has been long and anything but easy. This letter is written in the hope that you'll be able to look at this later and find comfort in knowing that what you haven't always known about me does not change who I am, my love and what we have always meant to each other.

I was sixteen when I finally accepted the truth. It was the summer between junior high and my freshman year of high school. I was aware that my friends were much more interested in dating. I wanted to date too! But only because they were doing it! About the same time I became increasingly aware of my physical attraction for men and the accompanying lack of any comparable interest in women. This is not to say I am not interested in women emotionally. As you both know I have always maintained strong relationships with many women. Pursuing this train of thought came further insight into previously repressed and misunderstood feelings from way back. This simple analysis indicated something undeniably significant. Many months followed attempting to understand this new awareness, it's cause and future ramifications.

At first the image of an unconventional life not confined by the usual restrictions of a family seemed an exciting alternative. It was soon that I discovered the negative aspects of an opposing lifestyle and its upcoming struggle. I was often depressed and thought many times of telling you and many times almost did. But, instinctively I knew you did not have the knowledge or experience to effectively confront this issue any better than I did. I knew you would answer with the ideas of counseling. Which I was strong enough of mind to know it would not change anything but perhaps only help us all to cope with the forthcoming stress and tension. Besides I decided I did not want a childhood stigmatized in this manner. My first year of high school when I was working on all this, I found myself more and more alienated from my friends, probably because I wasn't very comfortable with myself and because they were all investigating relationships when I met and started to date Hat ice. This made me feel more comfortable with my friends and my last two years of high school were made much easier. But I felt guilty using Hatice in this way. Our intimacy was satisfactory and I liked her very much as a person, although I wasn't physically attracted to her. I felt that she should have been with someone who could have appreciated her fully. This guilt made me feel very uncomfortable and I realized that I could never be happy pretending to be something I wasn't with anyone. This meant I needed to fully explore what form my life must take on.

In college, the dating issue did not have the same significance. Unlike many of the peer pressure that were so important in high school. It now seemed to dissipate while people found that their focus was not primarily themselves. In college I learned that no one should care what anyone else was doing and that I really didn't care if they did anyway. I had yet to act upon any of my inclinations and was both frightened and compelled. At this time I found it necessary to become vague and generally evasive about friends you could not know and places you knew nothing about. Eventually I told my good friend Cathie and she accepted me and gave me the support I so desperately needed. I started to understand that there was no reason that I could not function like anyone else and live a rewarding life with self-respect. I realized that being gay meant anything you wanted it to mean. If you perceived yourself as a healthy, happy person then so you are and likewise the reverse could be true. As in so many things it is your perception of self that really matters. Cathie remarked when I told her that she was surprised but, really relieved too! She always felt something about me had been unclear without an idea as to what it was. Which is I am sure much how you both have felt too! Much has happened since then, many memories too complexed and too personal to recount here but, I will tell you both anything you'll hear with an open mind.

I've been searching all along for a life-love partner. I've experimented with several relationships, none just right so far. I believe that it is possible for two men to create a nurturing, happy life together and it is to this goal that I strive. My life since that summer has been more difficult than if this had not happened-constantly guarding my thoughts and action with both of you, friends and associates. This difficulty has been because there are no conventional role models to provide inspiration, only shallow, unrealistic stereotypes. I have to still discover these things for myself. This rather quickly brings you up to date. Life finds me living out in San Francisco a whole year. I am as happy here as possible considering how much I enjoy what money affords. Hopefully I will find a rewarding job that will be financially satisfying too! I think I am becoming more realistic and at the same time developing patience. Also I am beginning to make progress in a more directed fashion toward my career. The turmoil, and settling of this move now behind me. I am hopeful.

I moved here for many reasons which I have shared with you. But what I did not share with you is my happiness in how comfortable I feel living here. A gay person here is much like a Cuban living in Miami. It simply does not matter to these people who are more real and honest with themselves and others. Maybe it is only because they have no choice but to relate with what constitutes a large sizable portion of this population. An active gay community thrives here with business guilds, athletic clubs, music and art organizations, etc. People meet in the usual ways here unlike cities across the country with only night clubs providing camaraderie. It is my hope that because of this more conducive atmosphere I will increase my opportunity to find a more meaningful relationship then I have found in the past. So, you see, San Francisco meets many of my needs. However, I do not know that this will always be so.

It has never been my intention to be distant from you. I do think that a change in our relationship was needed at this point in my life, because I so desperately need to become self-sufficient. I believe it has taken me so long because of my wish to be as much like what you would have wanted me to be. I did this consciously and often unconsciously in order that when you did find out about me you would at least feel consoled that I had measured up to most of your expectations. In April, last year at the airport, leaving Florida, I cried uncontrollably for at least a half an hour after dad had left. Suddenly it was very clear how silly it was for me to have ever considered living my life according to a perception of anyone else's expectation, no matter what were the underlying intentions. Of course, no one is to blame for any of this and as for your responsibility for my sexuality, you are I think as much responsible for that as you are responsible for my artistic ability! I hope you understand that there has never been a choice, if there had been it should have been an obvious one. This is simply the way it is and life is just too short to agonize over matters of act. I look forward for our time together and the opportunity for us to continue to grow in our lives with our love for each other.

All my love,
Brian

After the reading of the letter, we just knew we loved him and that we needed to support his decisions. We began to have more talks together and had more planned time together.

To have experienced this revelation, to have witnessed the man I married, his father, express such depth of love and compassion for me - as well as for our son - was truly a blessed moment. Our lives could have been shattered, but the strength and wisdom he showed was truly admirable. To have alienated our son would have devastated both our relationships; instead Albert made it possible for us all to grow in love as we learned how to understand the journey. Many family relationships have been destroyed by such bitterness, but we decided that together with God's help, we would evolve as a family.

This was a giant step for my wonderful husband. We grew up during a time when there was no tolerance or understanding of homosexuality. Our generation used slurs like queers, fairies, and worse. To understand the need for love and give unconditional love is true grace. I must admit when we went back home to Florida, after I had time to reflect on what was now a certainty, the days that followed were difficult. With much prayer and God's help, with some counseling and our love for each other, our aching hearts were eased.

The lack of choice is evident; homosexuals are born this way. Brian said to me once, "If I had a choice, mom, do you really think I would choose this way of life?" He was a gift from God, not to be abandoned but to be loved, supported, and understood. For a parent to abandon a child because of a sexual orientation is unforgivable. My heart aches for the many children who have been deserted by their families and are forced to go on this journey all alone.

CHAPTER 3

Effect on the Family

Robert, his brother, was so relieved when Brian was able to come out to him and his wife. It took courage for Brian to take this step, but Robert and Donna were not surprised. They had quite a few friends who are gay and they accepted Brian for who he was. They kept his secret for several years, and when he was finally able to tell us, they were very glad.

I must say that this revelation was no easy thing for me to accept. I felt such sadness that Brian would not have a typical family life: being married, fathering children. I felt he was so cheated. He was such a great person, with such compassion and understanding, I thought he would make such a wonderful husband and father. But I came to learn so much from him, and other homosexuals. They are more willing to show their feelings and don't feel it is wrong to let them show. I feel they are here to help all men learn about tenderness, and gentleness, which is against so many men's learned attitudes.

But my initial sadness was very deep; I fell into a depression, struggling with my lack of understanding. The why did this happen to my son? I was in despair, I was angry, I was tired. In my disbelief, I read books on the subject and learned enough to believe that his homosexuality wasn't my fault. I consulted with learned people. I prayed a great deal, asking for God to open my heart, for a way to understand the lessons in all of this. Many times, I was in such despair I thought if only I were dead I wouldn't have to face this lesson; I even contemplated suicide, but through my faith I found strength to believe that God would provide the way to understanding. I found myself growing more in love, not judgment.

Albert was sad for Brian, that this was to be his life, but was glad Brian had the courage to tell us. Albert was there for me, and together we consoled each other.

CHAPTER 4

God's Gifts

I have learned that for each of us the most precious gift is our life; God gives us free will to choose our path, and the path will lead us back to our creator. Each of us must find our own way. My mother, my greatest teacher, had a saying in her native tongue: *jeder wurt salic bei seiner eigenen haut*, which translates as "each becomes holy or enlighten by his own insight."

I believe that the experiences, the journey each of us has to undertake for our personal growth, leads to the ultimate graduation of a higher self.

We have many teachers to lead us along the pathway, first parents, then family, teachers, clergy, and all those we meet.

For me God has been an ever-present factor; I was raised Lutheran, sang in the choir, taught Sunday school, was the vice president of mother's club at church, attended bible class regularly, saw to it that our two sons were baptized, confirmed, had daily bible readings at supper time when the boys were small. Both of us were active parents in our church home for many years. Our sons, as they grew up, broke away from the church as many do, but I believe if they are exposed to church teachings when small they will return. We never forced our sons; they wanted to go. Faith and believing in the hereafter in my life has been strong and it is what has carried me through.

Our church experiences were opening our hearts and mind. The Bible says, "judge not, least ye be judged."

As a family, we would not have come thru our experience with Brian as well as we did were it not for our religious teachings, and our strong family foundation.

Where is it that we learn the basic rules for the journey of life? Isn't it in the home of our beginnings? When we learn those rules, how many of us are experience the loving, understanding, compassionate guidance that is so necessary for a fruitful, fulfilling life? How many of us carry into adulthood the inadequacy of the family household rules? How many of us come from dysfunctional homes? How many of us come from solid foundations?

There is no rulebook for bringing up children, except for the Bible or Torah. Each of us brings our particular values from our own beginnings, and we duplicate and multiply the systems and the windows of belief. Parents set the stage for the life journey, and it's no wonder that there are so many misfits or deeply wounded people. On the journey of life, each person has to find their own way into the light or the purpose of life. Each has in his or her power the control of action and thoughts; therefore, to judge another is so wrong as we are not equipped with someone else's set of rules. I guess that's where the saying 'do not judge another 'til you walk a mile in his shoes' originates.

Even though there are many different kinds of values, ethnic backgrounds, etc., we all need the same basic elements to be happy. We need respect for ourselves, for others, and from others. We need a purpose for life, and we need love - love to be given and love to be received.

I believe that is how to make sense of so many different nationalities and social cultures. That is why there are so many kinds of people: clergy, doctors, gamblers, judges, lawyers, police, poor, priest, rich, teachers. They are all trying to fulfill a need. How many times have you heard a doctor say he turned to his profession because of someone who had a particular illness in his family, or how he himself had some illness? We all continually work out those needs, whether they originate in hurt or in love. We learn through expressions of our words and actions.

If we could only realize the great responsibility each of us has as parents, we could understand that being given a child to nurture is a very precious gift and a huge responsibility. Values must be taught; compassion, honesty, humility, charity, perseverance, and respect must shown by example. Young minds are so impressionable. Thoughtless words said over and over, like you're stupid, you never can do that, you're too small, too big, too fat, or even constant reprimands damage a young mind for life. I was punished when small by sitting on stool in a dark cellar. It made me fearful of the dark for a long time. Some seek out psychologists to help sort out their problems, but many can't afford help and that is how society perpetuates such destructive beliefs.

At the holidays with our loved ones, there is no other time when the family ties are so evident. The rules of each family unit, of different spouses, is so strongly displayed. These exchanges of learned family values, often so varied, can cause such discomfort and such judgmental behaviors.

I believe until we realize the very basic needs, love and respect that each of us wants, we have not learned the rules of life. Many attitudes are so judgmental and why do we judge? Because our own basic family foundations are so varied and so different.

Technology has integrated the world. I believe we are to learn from another; we can all be one big family. If it was not so, why then aren't we all the same color, the same religion, the same nationality, all of one mind? Why are there so many kinds of animals, plants, and environments if we were not to learn and make choices?

The lack of understanding is what causes so much hurt and pain, creating big obstacles on the journey of life. If we cannot understand the basic needs in a family unit, where each member gets to know the other members better than an outsider, is it any wonder that nations do not respect and understand different cultural norms? We all have and need roots, and most importantly we are all God's children. When things don't go right, we hear the blame put on the childhood: I had a difficult childhood, they didn't understand me, etc.

Family relationships are so important; parents are the first contact we make as we come into this world. This first impression must be nurtured. Then siblings, they often become the real trial. When there is no nurturing foundation, poor choices are made. We, the parents, must ask ourselves - what and how are we relating to our children? Are we creating a healthy environment for their growth? Are we open-minded? Are we allowing the growth of each child? Are we setting good standards, or none at all? Are we bringing in old, destructive windows of belief? Are we helping their full self-worth?

The first seven years of a child are the formative years. Teach a child early in life the love of God, life, music, and nature.

Children Learn What They Live

If a child lives with criticism, he learns to condemn.

If a child lives with ridicule, he lives to be shy.

If a child lives with encouragement, he learns confidence.

If a child lives with praise, he learns to appreciate.

CHAPTER 5

The New Journey

Our young son moved to San Francisco after working as a stock broker in Florida. This was difficult for him to do, as we were so close a family and he would be so far from his parents and his brother.

It was a very brave move for Brian, and he was determined to make it work. He finally found another stock company in San Francisco and was content with his job. He had a great flair for writing and he began writing a newsletter for his associates which was circulated through the company. He made some special friends and found a young man who would begin to mean a great deal to him and eventually to all of us.

Little by little, he began to expose us to this young man he had chosen. Building a relationship was uncomfortable at first. We loved our young son so much and wanted to understand what he wanted us to know about himself and Mark. It wasn't easy to put aside all the preconceived notions, all the fault-finding and blaming.

Slowly, with time, we grew to realize that Mark was a very special person. He is a quiet, tender man and was reticent to involve himself with us, as he was afraid of how we would feel about him, or about our son's relationship with him. Our young son, wise and intelligent, helped us learn about Mark, and we found ourselves liking and respecting him, realizing that he genuinely cared for our son and his welfare.

To learn to accept all this was difficult to say the least, but through it all we realized that Brian had been our gift from God. Being our son, he was ours to love unconditionally.

Our son was born with the great gift of giving much joy and love to others. When he was little, my prayers were do not ever let me daunt the beautiful spirit of my son. My prayers were well-answered, as he lived for 35 years offering compassion and caring and love for all those who crossed his path. He had many friends, all ages, young and old, men and women, and they all loved him.

Brian was such an elegant man. He had so many dreams that were left unfilled. He envisioned a home in the upper part of California, in the mountains, with a Japanese-style garden with a pond, just like the one he would visit in the Golden Gate Park.

He and Mark had rented a lovely apartment from a police captain, who had left a garden unattended. Our son discovered beautiful calla lilies, almost five feet tall. We both loved calla lilies and they became a symbol for our family. He also had a great flair for design, just like his older brother, who had become a successful architectural designer. Even Brian's Christmas packages were works of art. He had a real talent for drawing and we are fortunate that we have some of them still hanging in our home. His eye for beauty was so great and he always selected such wonderful gifts for everyone. I have a beautiful musical jewelry box he gave me before he died, and it still plays "Till the End of Time" by Perry Como.

I didn't understand that selection of music until he was gone. It was his way of telling he would always be with me:

> *Till the end of time, long as stars are in the blue / Long as there's a Spring of birds to sing I'll go on loving you / Till the end of time, long as roses bloom in May / My love for you will grow deeper with every passing day / Till the wells run dry and each mountain disappears / I'll be there for you to care for you through laughter and through tears / So take my heart in sweet surrender and tenderly say that I'm the one you love and live for till the end of time*

He also sent us his last gift on April 1992, two months before his death, a beautiful flower arrangement from Hawaii for our anniversary. We dried it and will treasure it forever.

The man in his life, the man who gave meaning to his life, would heal the big gap in the bridge that held us all together. His experience with our son was one of growth for Mark; he developed self-confidence, gained maturity, and developed the ability to share his feelings. He learned he could trust us and we him.

The relationship between two people where your child is involved, this child who you so lovingly raised, now to be in the care of this other person, is difficult at the best of times. Trying to cope with all these new circumstances was a real test, but this young man proved to be the right partner for our young son. He was able to show love and compassion and we grew to love him. We are both grateful for the love Mark was able to give. To think of Brian dying without ever knowing love would be so much more painful.

CHAPTER 6

The Time Bomb

Brian changed jobs; he was working at an auction house as auction project manager. We were able to come to California and be near him for months at a time. For Christmas of 1990, we went out and stayed at a hotel.

He and his partner bought a Christmas tree and decorated it and put it in our room before we arrived. They also prepared a special dinner and had presents under the tree and a fire in the fireplace. We went caroling in the streets and then back to their apartment to open gifts.

Our young son decorated extensively, with boughs strung over the fireplace. I had misgivings, as they looked so dry. When the boughs caught on fire, he tore at them to push them into the fireplace. It was so scary. The tree could have gone up in flames so easily. Sparks had already melted the wrappings on the packages under the tree. His partner came to the rescue, putting out the fire with the fire extinguisher. Brian became hysterical. He said he had ruined everything. I was simply grateful that he hadn't been burned. He had a sweater on that could have caught on fire and he would have been in a hospital. This was not the end of the journey yet.

Looking back, I think about how fortunate we were to have had these times together. It is so important to be able to give love, to say the things that need to be said and not to hold back.

The following October our eldest son came to do an architectural rendering for our home in Florida. We had planned to go on a cruise. We had talked our younger son to coming with us for a week and so we asked the older one to come also. The brothers shared a room together, something they hadn't done in years. Needless to say, it was a great experience for us as a family. Our older son felt he could not stay the full week so he left us at Haiti and we continued on into the Caribbean. I know he wishes he had stayed with us, but hindsight is always better. We needed to create mementoes and savor each and every one. These precious memories will live with us forever.

The time bomb was ticking.

Brian went through so much symptomatic pain in the eight years he struggled with HIV: fevers and sweats, mouth thrush, shingles, but he never had to stay in a hospital overnight. He tried many treatments, including AZT. There were never any non-prescription drugs involved. He embraced a lot with holistic measures, and he was careful with his diet. He was seeing a doctor, the head of AIDS treatment at the San Francisco General Hospital, who took a special interest in him. He gave him encouragement and hope. He had given up smoking so his T cells were around 700; he was doing vitamin therapy. His discipline was good at this time.

Life seemed to be stable and he was adjusting to the challenges. We spoke on the phone many times a week and prayed together when the fear overwhelmed him. He loved to entertain and he and Mark were both wonderful cooks. By this time our family had grown; our eldest son Robert had married and now had a son. We were all invited, our family and his partners' family, out to San Francisco for Thanksgiving of 1991. The dinner was superb. Brian and Mark out-did themselves with their epicurean dinner. Family relationships were good and our son was in his glory. Brian also decorated the house beautifully. He even put up a wigwam for our grandson Matt to play in, because he was an Indian for Halloween. Brian was such a great uncle. He and Matt would play in our pool for hours when we would get together for holidays.

Our son planned every detail, even giving his brother a wonderful itinerary before their arrival in San Francisco.

He also planned a beautiful evening out, for the family - dinner and the opera. We all dressed formally and he had a professional photographer to capture this special evening for posterity. We will always remember that special evening. Looking back now, it was as if he knew this would be the last time for all of us to be together.

CHAPTER 7

The Time Bomb is Still Ticking

After Christmas, things began to change. Brian had gone back to smoking and his T-cells dropped to 20. One day after Christmas he called me; he thought his eyesight was changing, and he started to have headaches. I called the Miami hot-line for AIDS and they told me if that was the case he could go blind and would need intravenous injections permanently.

I started more fervent prayers. I had bought beautiful pitched wind chimes and had hung them outside and when the wind would blow it was like a call to arms. I would pray please let this cup pass from him. For him to lose his eyesight would have been devastating. To all of us it became apparent that he could no longer keep working, so he took disability. At this point I think he began to feel he was coming to his end; he tried to alienate his partner, thinking that it would spare him. But Mark, being the fine caring man he was, could not desert him. I think Brian decided to give up because he stopped taking his vitamins and medications. The AIDS had started to go to his brain, which in his case was a blessing. He really didn't know what was happening. Little by little, changes were taking place. He was finding it difficult to walk, as the muscles in his legs were getting weaker and he was having more headaches.

We decided it would be good to go on a family cruise and chose the Disney cruise ship, thinking it would be great fun for our little grandson. We certainly enjoyed being together but there were definite signs things were not going well. Our son would try to speak and things would come out all jumbled. Nevertheless, we were all grateful for our time together as a family

In March of 1992, Albert and I flew out to San Francisco and the three of us went to his favorite place, the Japanese tea garden in the Golden Gate Park. It was so beautiful there, with the azaleas in full bloom. For me it was hard not to show my fears. Brian was beginning to lose more muscle strength in his legs and found it very tiring to walk, but with grateful hearts we languished in our togetherness.

By May, his partner Mark felt that they should come to us in Florida as our son was having real difficulties.

Brian was having epileptic-type seizures, and he would bite his tongue severely. He would need to go to the hospital for dosages of Dilantin. They arrived Friday afternoon, and the air flight triggered another seizure the following morning. Brian had bit his tongue so severely that it was difficult for him to eat or talk, even though he remained his lovable sweet self even in pain. A trip by ambulance to the hospital was necessary.

We were all so aware that these were signs of his eminent death. An old friend of his came to visit him while he was in Florida. I saw our son down on our dock by the river. He was standing and saying his farewell to our home and his friend.

Soon after returning to California his ability to walk by himself became impossible, and Brian started to fall, so he needed care and Mark arranged for hospice to come. They were so good to him and said he was such a loving patient, never losing his temper or showing anger to anyone. Fearing that the end was near, we flew out to be with our son.

Our flight was delayed and this caused stress for him; he had another seizure in the morning. A close friend of his came from Texas to help us all through these last days. This Texas friend had been through this with several of his other friends. The morning found us all at the hospital, Brian was having bladder failure and when we brought him home he was put on a catheter.

Being with him in his final days was so difficult, to helplessly watch as he succumbed to AIDS, to this devastating disease. He was in his own bed and we prayed together many times. He said to me, "Mom, I am going to die?"

And I answered him and said, "Yes, I know."

He said, "You do."

To say those words out loud was so difficult, because it meant I had to acknowledge what was happening. I still don't know how I had the strength to utter them. I prayed the twenty-third psalm and the Apostle's Creed so many times as he came in and out of consciousness.

On Thursday I went shopping for some special food to make for him, and I made some comment about my hair, how it didn't look too good, and he said, "you're beautiful."

His sweet and beautiful nature was still there, and he managed to say something thoughtful to me even as he was dying. I will always treasure those words. They are imprinted on my heart.

His brother Robert was away at a convention and arrived on Friday evening. When he arrived, Brian was semi-conscious and in moments would try to talk, but he could only manage whispers, as his vocal chords had lost their dexterity. His forehead was so strained in appearance, the blood vessels protruding as he tried to talk. He wanted to say so much but he couldn't. His forehead relaxed when his brother came and talked with him. It was as if he knew we were all there with him.

He slipped deeper into unconsciousness. Saturday, he had a visitor, a gal, and she came to be with him for a while and shook him so he acknowledged her presence. Sunday, the doctor came and said his pulse was wild but that he had a strong heart and didn't know how long he would be in this state.

His brother decided to fly home to Michigan, as Brian had now slipped into deep unconscious and could be in this state for a while. In the morning as we were preparing to take Robert to the airport the call came that Brian had slipped away. We went to his bedside and said our tearful good-byes, and then the three of us went to the Japanese teahouse that he loved so much and had our last tea for him there.

CHAPTER 8

The Time Bomb Exploded

We were staying at a condo by the ocean, and in the aftermath planned the memorial for Saturday, as his partner Mark could not take off from work. Brian's death was not considered family for him.

My husband and I were in such a distraught state, all alone as Robert had to go home, no friends to console us; I could not see how we would make it through this long week. I have had a small devotional book called "The Quiet Mind" that has helped me always. I had given it to Brian but his partner gave it back to me the morning Brian died. I always prayed before I thumbed through it, that I would be guided to the page necessary for my contemplation. So I turned to it and "the hidden blessing" appeared:

Behind every dark happening, man has to develop faith and confidence in God, knowing that at the right moment, at the acceptable time of the Lord, the magic will be worked, the dark shroud will fall away and the radiant angel will be waiting. Behind all is the glory of God's life - the divine magic which illuminates all life's happenings.

This reading sustained us through this long week, and has continued to do so for us both even now.

Our son's wishes were to be cremated and for his ashes would be scattered at our summer home in the lake. But first we held the memorial in San Francisco. We saw such love and caring from the many visitors at his home. The fact that he was gay never changed our deep love and devotion for him, and as we learned more about the camaraderie of his friends, the sensitive and caring ways of these highly educated men and women, we began to see and understand their feelings.

His obituary read:

> *Brian slipped away peacefully of encephalopathy in his San Francisco home on June 22, 1992 at age 35. He is the beloved son of Albert and Inge of Stuart, Florida. He is survived by his special*

friend and partner, Mark, of San Francisco, California, beloved brother and sister-in-law and cherished nephew of Orchard Lake, Michigan.

At the memorial in San Francisco, we first gathered at Brian and Mark's home and then, with Mark and Albert at my side, some fifty of us walked to the pond at Golden Gate Park. This was Brian's special place where he would go to meditate. Poems were read and flowers were thrown in the pond as we reflected in silence of the terrible loss of our loved one. We returned back to their home where we chatted with many of their friends from all walks of life, sharing joyful moments and sad. It was the most stirring experience. These young people have had to deal with death of their friends in unbelievable numbers because of this terrible disease and they have been there for each other through all of the horrors of this terrible disease. Many have been abandoned by family. To me, that is unforgivable; it is a sin to isolate others from society. Our most merciful Father in heaven, I know, has compassion and mercy.

On the mantel of their home was a picture of Mark and Brian that had been painted by a dear artist friend, Bill. He had just finished the painted a few days before. He too is now deceased.

After arriving home in Florida, many of our friends came to share our loss; then our son wanted to have a memorial service in his church in Michigan. We arranged for Mark to fly in from California. The service was held on July 10, 1992 at the Orchard Lake Presbyterian Church with a very touching memorial by Pastor Hazelton and Pastor Fox. The urn with Brian's ashes, which Mark brought with him, was set at the altar, with a picture of Brian draped in black. There were many calla lilies.

The service began with Mark sitting on my left and Matt, my little grandson, on my right. There was a prayer first, and the reading of psalms, then our daughter-in-law sang "The Lord is My Shepherd," and then the reading of the New Testament passages. We sang the hymn "Our God, Our help in Age's Past," and then held the Resurrection homily before singing the hymn "Abide with Me."

These two pastors helped to assure us that a most merciful God would accept our son in his kingdom. Pastor Fox, who had confirmed our Brian at age 14, looked up his confirmation passage to recite. The Pastor read Isaiah 6:3: "And one cried unto another, and said, holy, holy, holy is the Lord of hosts: the whole Earth is full of his glory."

The memorial services help us to say goodbye.

Pastor Hazelton says, "who then can separate us from the love of Christ? The very nature of Christ that he pours out his godliness to be in the midst of us. By the stable, the rough wood of the cross, the smell of the sawdust, a fish in wood fires, dying is not a unique judgement on someone. You don't blame you don't blame people because they die even the unique disease or circumstance of their death. Christ sees the person. He knows the suffering. He sees the person."

He states the facts I gave him about Brian, born October 28, 1956, baptized at St. Olaf Church, Detroit, confirmed at St. John Lutheran Church, Farmington and that I, his mother, gave him a few opinions and he said, "one hit me like a stone." He was an elegant man whose joy came from giving joy to others. He was valiant to the end, never losing his sweet nature. Pastor said he got the picture. Never knowing him he said, "I know him, wish I had known him. Who wouldn't want to know to know someone who gets joy of giving other joy? A sweet-natured man who actually listened to you. He was baptized, confirmed. He took communion in his last days - Christ knows him. Christ smiles at his greeting. Weeps at his pain."

He went on to say "who can separate us from the love of Christ? Can trouble or hardship or persecution or peril or can danger, death, AIDS, in all these things we have complete victory through him that who loved us, who is in the midst of us and does not walk around us? So to Albert and Inge, to give Bob and Donna and Matt and Mark, we join with you in thisgoodbye to Brian and we pray God Christ his gentle soul to keep. Remember Matthew 7:1-3: 'judge not, lest ye be judged.'"

I wrote him a letter in gratefulness:

Dear Pastor Hazelton,

We felt so fortunate to have met you prior to the memorial service for our son, Brian. We felt your loving heart and knew it would be right for us to have the service at your church. These are difficult days for clergy and parishioner alike. So many issues but those standing in judgement will also have to answer to God. Thank you for your inspiring and comforting thoughts. To be in God's house was blessing indeed. We have learned much in our 44 years of marriage. Our son taught us much about unconditional love. I was so blessed having him for a son and also blessed with a wonderful husband who was a loving supportive father from the first day of Brian's revelation to us. Brian's revelation was very despairing for him as he was not how we would react and he also found it so difficult a life at first, then he met Mark. We came to love Mark very much as his tender caring for Brian was very special, a very gentle compassionate person. We witness upon the memorial gathering in San Francisco at Brian's home such caring, such compassion and such love as we have never seen in the heterosexual community. There is so much pain and loss of their friends, and they've learned they are alone against the world of such little understanding. Brian had lost ten friends and three at the gathering were HIV positive. We again thank you for providing deep feeling of gratefulness.

My letter to Pastor Fox:

Dear Pastor,

Albert and I want to thank you so much for the part took in the memorial service for Brian. It was so thoughtful of you to go back to records of many years ago to find the memory verse Brian had to offer at his confirmation. We have learned much since our earlier days and Brian has taught us much. I remember at St. John's Bible classes and a study of love. I have always remembered that.

After sharing time with friends at the church, we drove up to Charlevoix. We chartered a boat that would take us in front of our summer home. We lovingly said prayers and Mark scattered Brian's ashes in the lake; our grandson took the calla lilies and let them float towards shore. Thus ended our farewell to our beloved son.

CHAPTER 9

The Mourning is Forever

The loss is forever, time softens the pain and in time you remember only the beauty of moments shared.

The loss if forever, time softens the pain and in time you remember only the beauty of moments shared.

Our family usually got together at our home in Florida at Easter time and for Thanksgiving. We always centered our vacation time around with family work obligations, and as our daughter-in-law Donna was a school teacher, we worked around school schedules. Thanksgiving was always a double celebration as we had Thanksgiving on Thanksgiving Day with the usual church attendance and a bountiful Thanksgiving dinner, then on Friday we would celebrate our Christmas because we couldn't be together then.

We shared our daughter-in-law with her family in Milwaukee. In Florida, Christmas decorations would go up before everyone arrived, and all the shopping and wrapping of packages were done before the celebration.

Thanksgiving of 1992 was not going to be easy for us all without Brian, so we decided to go to Disney World; we had to consider our grandson, Matt, who was now six years old and we felt this would be best for all of us. No decorations were put up and we made the best of it at Disney. It seemed so odd there, especially eating dinner out alone, which had not happened in 44 years. It was difficult but we knew Brian was with us in spirit.

By Easter time in 1993, we came together again and flowers were blooming in our garden. I had cultivated a Japanese garden with a small fountain on the south side of our home by the river. In May of 1992, just before Brian died, he and Mark came to visit us and they brought calla lily bulbs for me. Of course, I planted them and on the morning of Easter 1993 one single calla lily fully bloomed.

To us, this was a sign that Brian was there with us. That lily never bloomed again.

We keep his pictures all over the house, and I know he is with us always. On his birthday in October we burn a candle and have a bouquet of calla lilies in the house and the same in June, on the day he left us. I feel keeping all the memories alive sustain us. We had many difficult days adjusting to our loss. I perhaps fared better than his father Albert, as I could cry. I also died a little each day, knowing we could lose him, from the day we learned of his affliction with HIV.

For the first year, Albert was in a state of denial, of just not accepting Brian's death. He had pushed his pain away and tried to go on with normal living. Men don't handle death the way women do because we give birth and know the delicate thread that hangs between life and death. The second year was worse for him. He went into depression and was not coping. He couldn't seem to handle his daily affairs.

I found talking about it eased my pain. Telling people of Brian's struggle with AIDS helped me. Albert suffered severe neck problems. His neck has always been his weak spot. He couldn't seem to hold his head up for very long. And he had two spells where he fell backwards without warning, flat on his back. After these falls, of course we sought medical advice. After all the necessary tests, MRIs, etc., the doctors decided that these symptoms were all brought on by his emotional state.

Albert started biofeedback therapy to help him live with the neck pain and then sought out counseling to help him accept Brian's death, which was a step in the right direction. It took him three years after Brian's death to start thinking in the present. It was difficult to see Albert that way, but we all have to grieve in our own way. We must be allowed to grieve. It is a necessary path to healing. Thank God we could talk to each other about our loss, the pain and anguish we felt.

The business we were in gave us an opportunity to be in front of many people and Albert was able to say in their presence that he lost his son. That was the good part of therapy for him; to be able to acknowledge out loud was necessary for his emotional health. Into the fourth year, I gradually saw his great energy returning. He admitted to me that he really hadn't felt like doing anything in his office for the past three years. He would go in and shuffle and put them in boxes in corners. He maintained a survival attitude or a 'time will help' attitude. Our son Robert also felt a need for counseling.

It is true when they say time heals but the loss will always be with you. That we shared wonderful loving times together as a family and that we gave love and support has helped us through the many sad days. The reason I felt it so necessary to write this story was to share our experience, hoping to inspire those who have not been able to open their hearts. To know that where there is love, everything can be endured.

CHAPTER 10

About AIDS

I believe this horrendous disease, which is afflicting so many, heterosexuals included, is not understood by the masses and perhaps it's God's way of showing us how much we are all interrelated. That each action, each situation is linked, that each ripple each pebble of sand is connected. That we cannot be separate.

We live in a world that takes much of life for granted. What a precious gift from God, a child, a child to nurture. What a huge responsibility. This is why a mother and father are necessary to provide a secure and loving environment. Young minds are so impressionable. Young minds can so easily be damaged, as is evident in society around the world. All of us are different and yet we all need love, respect, and understanding. The ultimate lesson here is the awareness of the need for love - love for all of us. To learn to love is the essential reality, and our purpose here on Earth for all.

It has been some time since I started to write about our journey. I have now reached the age of 89, almost 90. It has been 25 years now since Brian's death. The journey has been difficult at times but I have learned that the challenges are there to strengthen us. My belief in the higher power I call God has been my strength for this journey.

It isn't easy to believe in a higher power, but for me it is so evident. The very fact of conception - the miracle that can happen as often as it does - where a being takes on the genes of his parent, becomes an extension of that union, is proof enough that this mighty maker of heaven and Earth helps preserve and protect all his creatures and creations.

The higher power has provided us with a great capacity for knowledge. We all must walk the journey alone to the final place of judgement day, but there are guides along the way. I believe that nothing happens by accident; those lessons come by divine guidance with teachers along the way. The lessons many times are very painful and certainly not our choice. Free will comes in how we handle the lesson.

I believe each of us is born with a unique gift to give and each should have the right to find and be able to give it. So when we are rearing our children it should be uppermost in our mind to strengthen and support the self-worth of that being, to appreciate their life and purpose.

The learning process isn't easy. As children, we have to learn all the basics: Walk, talk, how to behave, how to have compassion and control. As parents, we teach and wait and learn. Most of us teach as we have been taught and that sometimes is the cause of our prejudices, our disbeliefs, because we are different and come from different cultures. The windows become distorted, because of jealousy and anger.

There are so many hate movements in the world today. Love is what heals. When there is love, there is openness, understanding, compassion and acceptance, no need for judgement. Love is not judgmental. To love and be loved is the greatest gift of all. The beauty in all of this journey was the opening of our hearts, just realizing the need to know we are loved and that we can give love. Isn't that the need that motivates us all?

Love transcends all understanding. The insight to be able to see that each encounter is not by chance but for our spiritual growth is true enlightenment.

CHAPTER 11

Reality vs. Fantasy

In our lives together, we choose to live in the present, maybe never taking time to reflect or look ahead. Little did I realize that it was all too much: the hour or moment of the beginning of the end. I always wanted to believe Brian would live forever, especially in trying to give him the food that would keep him with us.

Foolish me, it was May, his last time with us and I should have made him the biggest breakfast of all the things he loved. The creamy French waffle, the French pancake. Instead I made the oats cakes with whole grain, still thinking I had time to give him the nutrients that would make him live. He and Mark said they were good, but we all realized that it no longer mattered, the hour was soon at hand. Of course, we did not know how soon it would be. One month later he was gone out of our lives.

Hindsight is always available but it cannot change the past. I fully believe it is always the best to open your heart. You never know when it will be too late. Love is what we are born with fear is what we learn. The spiritual journey is the unlearning of fear and the acceptance of love back into our hearts. To learn to love is our purpose on earth.

Time has flown by. I have tried to write this story over many years.

It is 2017 and I am 89, married 69 years, raised two sons, and am now a great grandmother. I feel that God has always been there for me. The journey has been difficult at times but everyone has challenges or obstacles to overcome. They add strength to our character.

The need for prayer was always there but after Brian's passing, I felt a greater need to help me center again. It is so hard sometimes to formulate words of prayer. His loss is so hard to bear. The words he is gone are so hard to bear.

I have to let him go.

Printed in the United States
By Bookmasters